PHONE REPAIR

Manual for repairing your smartphone device

Complete Guide for All Smartphone Devices

Manual EN

INDEX

1 INTRODUCTION

1.2 Purpose of the Guide

The purpose of the guide is to provide step-by-step, step-by-step instructions for repairing Android and Apple phones. The main goal is to help users fix common hardware and software issues that can occur in mobile phones, allowing them to make repairs themselves. The guide aims to be a comprehensive resource, offering information on necessary tools, safety precautions, diagnosing problems, and step-by-step procedures for resolution.

Additionally, the guide could emphasize the importance of preventative maintenance and best practices to extend the life of your phone. The ultimate goal is to provide users with the confidence and skills needed to manage the maintenance and repairs of their devices, reducing reliance on technical support services and saving time and money.

1.3 Tools Needed.

The tools you need to repair Android and Apple phones depend on the type of work you intend to do. Here's a general list of tools that might be useful:

Dismantling kit:

Precision screwdrivers (Phillips, Torx, Pentalobe)
Plastic or metal opening spatulas
Anti-static tweezers
Suction cup to lift the screen

Diagnostic Tools:
Multimeter to check electrical continuity
Tools to detect short circuits
Battery Testing Tools

Soldering Tools:
Adjustable soldering station
Hot air soldering iron or heat gun
Solder paste and flux

Screen Replacement Tools:
New Replacement Screen
Adhesive to fix the screen
Anti-static gloves to protect components

Battery Replacement Tools:
Compatible replacement battery
Tool to open the battery compartment (if necessary)
Double-sided tape to secure the new battery
Connector Repair Tools:

New Replacement Connector
Connector Removal and Replacement Tools

Diagnostic & Backup Software:
Data Backup Software
Diagnostic programs specific to your phone model

Cleaning Tools:
Solvent for cleaning electronic boards
Antistatic brushes
Lint-free cloths

Be sure to tailor this list based on the specific needs of your guide and the type of repairs you plan to cover. In addition, it is always advisable to use high-quality tools and take all necessary precautions to avoid further damage during the repair.

1.4 Safety Precautions
Safety is a priority when repairing Android and Apple phones. Here are some precautions to take before you start:

Turning Off Your Phone:

Make sure the phone is completely turned off before starting the repair.

Static:

Wear an anti-static wristband to prevent damage from static electric shock.

Clean Working Environment:

Work in a clean, dust-free environment to avoid contamination.

Eye Protection:

Wear safety goggles to protect your eyes from splinters or small particles.

Personal Safety:

Avoid eating or drinking during repair to prevent contamination. Wash your hands before starting.

Safe welding:

Use safe welding equipment and follow safety regulations. Make sure the work area is well ventilated.

Appropriate Tools:

Use the correct tools to avoid damage to the phone's components or yourself.

Battery Isolation:

If you need to remove the battery, make sure it is completely insulated to prevent short circuits.

Follow the Manufacturer's Guidelines:

Consult your phone manufacturer's instructions and follow the recommended guidelines.

Backup Before Repair:

Make a full backup of your data before starting the repair to avoid the loss of important information.

Beware of Stickers:

Pay attention to adhesives that may have been used to seal your phone. Carefully remove them and, if necessary, replace them when reassembling.

Photographic documentation:

Take photos during each step of the repair to help during reassembly and in case you need to consult the manufacturer or seek online service.

Skills and Competences:

If an operation seems too complex, it is best to seek the help of professionals or authorized service centers.

Remember that safety is paramount, and it's important to be aware of potential risks when repairing. Don't hesitate to stop the operation if you have any difficulties or if you don't feel confident about a particular procedure.

2 DIAGNOSING THE PROBLEM

2.1 Identify symptoms

To diagnose problems with an Android or Apple phone, it's crucial to be able to identify the symptoms. Here are some tips on how to recognize common symptoms:

Screen Not Responding:

The touchscreen does not react to touches.

The display shows dead pixels, lines, or spots.

Power Supply Problems:

The phone won't turn on.

It turns off suddenly even though the battery is full.

Battery Problems:

Battery life is drastically reduced.

The phone also turns off with a percentage of battery remaining.

Charging Problems:

The phone won't charge or charges slowly.

The charging connector is unstable or damaged.

Faulty Audio:

No sound during calls.

Difficulty listening to music or notifications.

Connection Issues:

Problems with Wi-Fi or mobile data connection.

Bluetooth doesn't connect properly.

Software Issues:

Apps that freeze or close unexpectedly.

Blue or black screens.

General slowness of the system.

Camera Problems:

The camera does not open or close suddenly.

The image quality is poor or blurry.

Network Issues:

Inability to make or receive calls.

Network-related error messages.

Heating Problems:

The phone gets hot even under normal conditions of use.

Sudden shutdowns due to overheating.

Sensor Problems:

Proximity sensor not working during calls.

The brightness sensor does not adjust the brightness of the screen properly.

Memory Problems:

Memory full, despite few apps installed.

Out of memory messages when installing new apps.

To diagnose the problem, it is helpful to gather detailed information about the symptoms you are experiencing and the environment in which they occur. In some cases, observing when and how problems manifest themselves can help identify the underlying cause.

2.2 Using Diagnostic Tools

Using diagnostic tools can be essential for accurately identifying problems with an Android or Apple phone. Here's how you can use some common diagnostic tools:

System Diagnostics App:

Download and install system diagnostic apps from the respective App Store (e.g., for Android, you may use "Phone Doctor Plus" or "CPU-Z").

Run available tests for the CPU, RAM, battery, and other key components.

Analyze the results for anomalies or problems.

Battery Test:

Use specialized apps for battery testing (such as "AccuBattery" for Android).

Monitor battery health, remaining capacity, and pinpoint any charging issues.

Performance Monitoring App:

Install performance monitoring apps like "GSam Battery Monitor" or "CPU Monitor" for Android.

It monitors CPU usage, device temperature, and memory usage to identify possible overloads.

Wi-Fi Diagnostic Software:

If the problem is with Wi-Fi connectivity, use apps like "WiFi Analyzer" for Android to identify interference or signal issues.

Touchscreen Test:

Look for apps that allow you to test your touchscreen and sensors, such as "Touchscreen Test" for Android.

Check the touchscreen response, calibration, and accuracy.

Apple Diagnostic Tools:

For Apple devices, use diagnostic tools such as "Apple Diagnostics" or "Apple Configurator 2" on a Mac computer to perform extensive hardware testing.

Electronic Soldering Tools:

If the problem is related to electrical connections or soldering, a multimeter and a soldering diagnostic tool can be helpful in locating faulty connections or short circuits.

Network Monitoring App:

Use apps like "Network Analyzer" for Android to monitor network connectivity, identify connection issues, and measure data rates.

Software Recovery Tools:

For software issues, use tools like "iTunes" for Apple devices or "Android Data Recovery" to restore the software or recover data.

Online Diagnostic Tools:

Some manufacturers offer online diagnostic tools that can help identify specific problems. Check your phone manufacturer's website for more information.

Remember to interpret the results of diagnostic tools carefully and refer to the manufacturer's resources for proper interpretation. If you are unsure or if you are still having problems, it may be advisable to consult a specialized technician or the manufacturer's support.

3 REPAIRING COMMON HARDWARE
3.1 Replacing the Screen

Screen replacement is one of the most common hardware repairs for Android and Apple phones. Here's a step-by-step guide:

Warning: Before you begin, make sure you have the necessary repair tools and follow all safety precautions. If your phone is still under warranty, replacing the display may void the warranty.

3.1.1 Tools Needed:

Disassembly kit.

New compatible replacement screen.

Antistatic tweezers.

Precision screwdrivers (Phillips, Torx, Pentalobe).

Suction cup to lift the screen.

Anti-static cloth.

Double-sided tape to secure the new screen.

Procedure:

Turn off your phone:

Make sure your phone is completely turned off before you begin.

Removing the Back Cover:

If your phone has a removable back cover, remove it according to the manufacturer's instructions.

Remove the Battery (if possible):

If it's possible to remove the battery without damaging your phone, gently pry it out.

Disassemble the Phone:

Use the disassembly tools to open your phone carefully. Pay attention to the flexible connectors and use the spatula to gently separate the frame.

Disconnect the Faulty Display:

Find and disconnect the display connectors from the rest of your phone. Usually, there will be several connectors, including those for the touchscreen, the LCD display, and the proximity sensor.

Remove the Defective Display:

Carefully lift the defective display. You can use a suction cup to help you lift it. Be sure not to force and avoid damage to the flexible cables.

Installing the New Display:

Align the new display with your phone's frame and connect the connectors. Make sure they are well inserted.

Remove any protective films from the new display before continuing.

Reassembling the Phone:

Reverse the steps above to reassemble your phone. Make sure all connectors are reconnected properly.

Use double-sided tape to securely attach the new screen to the frame.

Turning on the Phone:

Turn on your phone and see if the new screen is working properly. Control touch response, brightness, and image quality.

Operational Verification:

Make sure all of your phone's features, including the touchscreen, camera, and sensors, are working properly.

Remember to consult guides specific to your phone model and follow the manufacturer's instructions carefully. If you don't feel confident doing the replacement yourself, consider going to a professional or service center.

3.1.2   Disassembly and Reassembly Steps

Here is a step-by-step guide for the steps of disassembling and reassembling when replacing the screen of an Android or Apple phone. Make sure you have all the necessary tools before you begin.

Disassembly:

Turn off your phone:

Make sure your phone is completely turned off before you begin.

Remove the Back Cover:

If your phone has a removable back cover, remove it according to the manufacturer's instructions.

Remove the Battery (if possible):

If the battery can be removed without damaging the phone, take it out.

Find Access Points:

Use an opener tool to find and open access points to your phone. They are usually located along the edge between the frame and the back cover.

Only the Screws:

Use precision screwdrivers to remove visible screws. Some phones may use screws of different sizes, so keep track of where they belong.

Lift the Front Cover:

Use a spatula to gently pry the front cover off the frame. Pay attention to flexible connectors.

Disconnect Connectors:

Find the connectors for the display, battery, and other electronics inside your phone. Disconnect them carefully using the anti-static tweezers.

Remove the Defective Display:

Carefully lift the defective display. You can use a suction cup to help you lift it. Be sure not to force and avoid damage to the flexible cables.

Disconnect Other Components (if necessary):

If the repair requires the replacement of additional components, such as the camera or proximity sensor, carefully unplug them.

Replacement:

Installing the New Display:

Align the new display with your phone's frame and connect the connectors. Make sure they are well inserted.

Remove any protective films from the new display before continuing.

Reconnect other components:

Reconnect the camera, proximity sensor, and other previously disconnected components if necessary.

Connect the Battery:

Reconnect the battery to your phone, if previously removed.

Reassembling the Phone:

Reverse the steps above to reassemble your phone. Make sure all connectors are reconnected properly.

Use double-sided tape to securely attach the new screen to the frame.

Put the Back Cover Back in Place:

Put the back cover back in place and make sure it's properly aligned. Retighten the screws, if any.

Turn on your phone:

Turn on your phone and see if the new screen is working properly. Control touch response, brightness, and image quality.

Operational Verification:

Make sure all of your phone's features, including the touchscreen, camera, and sensors, are working properly.

Remember to follow your phone manufacturer's instructions carefully and use high-quality tools to avoid damage in the process. If you have any doubts or uncertainties, it may be advisable to contact a professional technician or service center.

3.2 Battery Replacement

Replacing the battery is a relatively common operation to maintain your phone's performance. Here's a step-by-step guide to replacing the battery on an Android or Apple phone:

Battery Replacement on Android Phones:

Tools Needed:

Disassembly kit.

New compatible battery.

Antistatic tweezers.

Precision screwdrivers.

Plastic opening spatula.

Double-sided tape to secure the new battery.

Procedure:

Turn off your phone:

Make sure your phone is completely turned off before you begin.

Remove the Back Cover:

If your phone has a removable back cover, remove it according to the manufacturer's instructions.

Take out the Battery:

If the battery is removable, use the plastic opening spatula to carefully remove it.

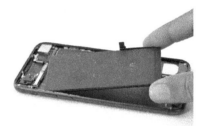

Measure the New Battery:

Measure the new battery to make sure it's compatible with your phone model.

Place the New Battery:

Place the new battery in the battery compartment, making sure it is seated correctly.

Reconnect the Battery:

Connect the new battery to the connector on your phone.

Secure the Battery with Double-Sided Tape:

Use double-sided tape to securely attach the new battery to your phone.

Reassembling the Phone:

Reverse the steps above to reassemble your phone. Make sure all connectors are reconnected properly.

Turn on your phone:

Turn on your phone and see if the new battery is recognized and working properly.

Battery Calibration:

Fully discharge the battery, then fully recharge it to properly calibrate the new battery.

Battery Replacement on Apple Phones:

Tools Needed:

Disassembly kit.

New battery compatible with disassembly tools.

Precision screwdrivers.

Antistatic tweezers.

Heat extractor or heat gun.

Double-sided tape to secure the new battery.

Procedure:

Check the Warranty:

Check to see if your phone is still covered by the warranty, as replacing the battery may void your warranty.

Turn off your phone:

Make sure your phone is completely turned off before you begin.

Remove the Back Cover (if necessary):

Some iPhone models may require the back cover to be removed. Follow the model-specific instructions.

Remove the Battery with the Heat Extractor:

Use the heat extractor or a heat gun to gently heat the perimeter of the phone and soften the adhesive holding the battery in place.

Use a plastic opening spatula to lift the battery carefully.

Reconnect the New Battery:

Connect the new battery using the anti-static tweezers. Make sure the connectors are securely inserted.

Secure the New Battery with Double-Sided Tape:

Use double-sided tape to securely attach the new battery to your phone.

Reassembling the Phone:

Reverse the steps above to reassemble your phone. Make sure all connectors are reconnected properly.

Turn on your phone:

Turn on your phone and see if the new battery is recognized and working properly.

Battery Calibration:

Fully discharge the battery, then fully recharge it to properly calibrate the new battery.

Remember to consult your phone manufacturer's specific guides and use high-quality tools to avoid damage in the process. If you have any doubts or uncertainties, it may be advisable to contact a professional technician or service center.

3.2.1 Battery Selection

Selecting the right battery is crucial to ensure optimal and safe operation of your phone after replacement. Here are some steps you can follow to select the suitable battery:

1. Check Your Phone Model:

Make sure you know the specific model of your phone. This information is usually found in your phone's settings or on its packaging.

2. Check the Original Battery Capacity:

Check your phone's original battery capacity. This information can be found in the settings or through diagnostic applications.

3. Look for a Compatible Battery:

Look for a replacement battery that is compatible with the specific model of your phone.
You can find replacement batteries online through reputable websites or at authorized dealers.

4. Read Battery Reviews & Reviews:

Before buying, read reviews and ratings about the specific battery you're considering. This will give you an idea of the quality and performance of the battery.

5. Compare Specifications:

Check the battery's technical specifications, including mAh (milliampere-hour) capacity, voltage, and compatibility. Make sure the new battery has at least the same capacity as the original one, or possibly a higher capacity for longer battery life.

6. Choosing Reliable Branded Batteries:

Prefer reliable and recognized brand batteries. Inferior batteries may not provide the desired performance and may present safety hazards.

7. Consider the Warranty:

Check to see if the replacement battery is covered by a warranty. A good warranty is a sign of confidence in the quality of the product.

8. Review the Return Policy:

Before making your purchase, review the seller's return policy in case the battery is found to be defective or incompatible with your device.

9. Beware of Safety Certification:

Check to see if the battery has safety certifications, such as CE or UL certifications, that indicate that the battery has undergone safety testing.

10. Professional Advice:

If you have any doubts or uncertainties, seek advice from professionals or specialized technicians. They can help you find the battery that best suits your needs.

Remember that choosing a quality battery is crucial to ensuring safe and reliable operation of your phone. Follow these guidelines and precautions to avoid future problems resulting from replacing the battery.

3.2.2   Replacement Procedures

Here's a step-by-step procedure for replacing the battery on an Android or Apple phone. This guide is generic, so it's important to also consult the specifications of your phone model and follow the manufacturer's instructions:

Battery Replacement Procedure:

Warning: Before you begin, make sure you have all the necessary tools and follow all safety precautions carefully. The steps may vary depending on the specific model of your phone.

Tools Needed:

Disassembly kit.

New compatible battery.

Antistatic tweezers.

Precision screwdrivers.

Plastic opening spatula.

Double-sided tape to secure the new battery.

For Android phones:

Turn off your phone:

Make sure your phone is completely turned off before you begin.

Remove the Back Cover (if necessary):

If your phone has a removable back cover, remove it according to the manufacturer's instructions.

Take out the Battery:

If the battery is removable, use the plastic opening spatula to carefully remove it.

Measure the New Battery:

Measure the new battery to make sure it's compatible with your phone model.

Place the New Battery:

Place the new battery in the battery compartment, making sure it is seated correctly.

Reconnect the Battery:

Connect the new battery to the connector on your phone.

Secure the Battery with Double-Sided Tape:

Use double-sided tape to securely attach the new battery to your phone.

Reassembling the Phone:

Reverse the steps above to reassemble your phone. Make sure all connectors are reconnected properly.

Turn on your phone:

Turn on your phone and see if the new battery is recognized and working properly.

Battery Calibration:

Fully discharge the battery, then fully recharge it to properly calibrate the new battery.

For Apple phones:

Check the Warranty:

Check to see if your phone is still covered by the warranty, as replacing the battery may void it.

Turn off your phone:

Make sure your phone is completely turned off before you begin.

Remove the Back Cover (if necessary):

Some iPhone models may require the back cover to be removed. Follow the model-specific instructions.

Remove the Battery with the Heat Extractor:

Use the heat extractor or a heat gun to gently heat the perimeter of the phone and soften the adhesive holding the battery in place.

Use a plastic opening spatula to lift the battery carefully.

Reconnect the New Battery:

Connect the new battery using the anti-static tweezers. Make sure the connectors are securely inserted.

Secure the New Battery with Double-Sided Tape:

Use double-sided tape to securely attach the new battery to your phone.

Reassembling the Phone:

Reverse the steps above to reassemble your phone. Make sure all connectors are reconnected properly.

Turn on your phone:

Turn on your phone and see if the new battery is recognized and working properly.

Battery Calibration:

Fully discharge the battery, then fully recharge it to properly calibrate the new battery.

Remember to consult your phone manufacturer's specific guides and use high-quality tools to avoid damage in the process. If you have any doubts or uncertainties, it may be advisable to contact a professional technician or service center.

3.3 Repairing Connectors

Repairing the connectors on a phone may be necessary if you are experiencing connection or functionality issues due to faulty connections. Here's a general guide on how to approach connector repair:

1. Symptom Assessment:

Identify symptoms that may indicate a problem with the connectors. These symptoms may include loss of connection, intermittent operation of a device, or a lack of response to a specific action.

2. Turn Off Your Phone:

Before starting any kind of repair work, make sure that your phone is completely turned off.

3. Tools Needed:

Disassembly kit.

Antistatic tweezers.

Precision screwdrivers.

Soldering iron (if necessary).

Rubber tape.

Thermal paste (if needed).

4. Isolation and Identification of the Defective Connector:

Isolate and identify the specific connector that is causing the problem. This requires opening the phone with the disassembly kit.

5. Cleanliness Check:

Examine the connector to make sure there is no debris, dust, or corrosion that could interfere with the connection. Clean gently with compressed air or a brush.

6. Reconnecting:

If the connector is disconnected, carefully plug it back in. Use anti-static tweezers to prevent static damage to components.

7. Welding (if necessary):

If the connector is damaged or sectioned, soldering may need to be performed. This requires welding skills and should be done very carefully to avoid damage to surrounding components.

8. Insulation with Electrical Tape:

If you've done a solder, or if you want to ensure that the connector stays securely in place, you can use electrical tape to secure it.

9. Functional Control:

Turn on your phone and see if the issue is resolved. Make sure all functions connected to the repaired connector are working properly.

10. Reassembling the Phone:

Reassemble your phone by following the steps in the disassembly kit.

11. Final Test:

Do a full test of your phone to make sure all features are back to normal.

Remember that repairing connectors may require technical expertise, especially if it involves soldering. If you don't feel confident going through the repair yourself, consider going to a specialized technician or service center. Also, remember to comply with safety regulations throughout the process.

3.3.1 USB, audio jack, etc.

Repairing USB connectors, audio jacks, and other types of connectors may be necessary when problems such as intermittent connections, lack of response, or distorted audio occur. Here's a general guide on how to approach the repair of these connectors:

1. Symptom Assessment:

Identify specific symptoms related to the connector, such as loss of connection, audio malfunction, or lack of device recognition.

2. Turn Off the Device:

Make sure the device is completely turned off before starting any repairs.

3. Tools Needed:

Disassembly kit.

Antistatic tweezers.

Precision screwdrivers.

Soldering iron (if necessary).

Rubber tape.

Possibly, compatible replacement connectors.

4. Isolation and Identification of the Defective Connector:

Isolate and identify the specific connector that is causing the problem. You may need to open the device with the disassembly kit.

5. Check Cleanliness:

Examine the connector to make sure there is no debris, dust, or corrosion that could interfere with the connection. Clean gently with compressed air or a brush.

6. Reconnecting:

If the connector is disconnected, carefully plug it back in. Use anti-static tweezers to prevent static damage to components.

7. Welding (if necessary):

If the connector is damaged or damaged, soldering may need to be performed. This requires welding skills and should be done very carefully.

8. Insulation with Electrical Tape:

If you've done a solder, or if you want to ensure that the connector stays securely in place, you can use electrical tape to secure it.

9. Functional Control:

Turn on your device and see if the issue is resolved. Make sure all functions connected to the repaired connector are working properly.

10. Reassembling the Device:

Reassemble the device by following the steps in the disassembly kit.

11. Final Test:

Carry out a full test of the device to ensure that all functionality is back to normal.

Important Notes:

Welding can be a delicate procedure and requires experience. If you don't feel confident, consult a professional.

Be sure to comply with safety regulations throughout the process.

If the connector is irreparably damaged, replacing it may be the best option.

Remember that repairing specific connectors may vary depending on the type of device and model, so also follow the manufacturer's instructions whenever possible.

3.3.2   Electronic Soldering

Electronic soldering is an essential skill for the repair and construction of electronic devices. Here's a basic guide on electronic soldering:

Tools Needed:

Soldering Station:

An adjustable soldering station allows you to set the correct temperature according to the needs of the job.

Soldering iron:

Use a quality soldering iron with a tip that fits the size of the component being soldered.

Flux:

The flux helps to clean surfaces and improve conductivity. It can be in paste or liquid form.

Welding:

It uses high-quality, lead-free solder, with a diameter suitable for the size of the job.

Antistatic tweezers:

Anti-static tweezers help to handle components safely.

Smoke Extractor or Welding Fan:

They reduce exposure to toxic vapors generated during welding.

Component Support:

A stand helps keep the component fixed while welding.

Cutter or Spatula for Cleaning:

Use to remove residual flux after soldering.

Multimeter:

Use to test electrical connectivity after welding.

Welding Procedure:

Preparation:

Make sure you work in a well-ventilated area.

Turn on the soldering station and set the correct temperature for the type of soldering and the components involved.

Cleaning the tips:

Wipe the tip of the soldering iron with a damp sponge to remove previous soldering residue.

Flux Application:

Apply flux to the area to be soldered to improve conductivity and facilitate soldering.

Heating of Components:

Touch the component and track with the soldering iron to heat them evenly.

Welding Application:

Apply solder to the heated area until it melts evenly and covers the connection.

Cooling:

Let the solder cool naturally without disturbing the connection.

Inspection:

Visually examine the weld to make sure it's even, with no solder bridges or cold joints.

Cleanliness:

Clean the surrounding area with a cutter or spatula to remove any residual flow.

Test:

It uses a multimeter to check electrical connectivity through soldering.

Tips:

Precision:

Be precise in the amount of solder used. Too much soldering can cause short circuits.

Proper Flux:

Use the right flux for the type of solder. Some fluxes require cleaning after soldering.

Soldering Tips:

Use clean, well-groomed soldering tips to ensure optimal conductivity.

Antistatic Protection:

Wear cuffs or rest your wrists on anti-static surfaces to prevent electrostatic damage to components.

Practice:

Practice on scrap components before tackling more complex devices.

Remember that practice is key to acquiring electronic soldering skills, and adherence to safety procedures is essential to prevent damage to components and ensure safe work.

3.4 Replacing the Physical Buttons

Replacing physical buttons on a device may be necessary if the buttons have issues such as unresponsiveness, unregistered clicks, or if they are physically damaged. Below, you'll find a general guide on how to replace physical buttons:

Tools Needed:

Disassembly Kit:

Includes precision screwdrivers, opening spatulas, and other necessary utensils.

New Replacement Buttons:

Make sure you have buttons that are compatible with your device.

Antistatic tweezers:

Useful for handling components without damaging them.

Instant Glue Tube or Double-Sided Adhesive:

To attach the new buttons.

Button Replacement Procedure:

Turn off the Device:

Make sure the device is completely turned off before starting any replacement operations.

Removing the Cover or Shell:

Use the disassembly kit to remove the cover or case of the device. This may require the use of precision screwdrivers or opening spatulas.

Inspection and Identification:

Inspect faulty buttons and identify how they are connected to the circuit board.

Removing Defective Buttons:

Use tweezers to carefully remove the faulty buttons. Make sure you don't damage the surrounding circuitry.

Cleanliness of the Zone:

Clean the area of debris from old buttons or any debris that may be interfering with the new buttons.

Installing the New Buttons:

Place the new buttons in their slots, making sure they are aligned correctly.

Fixing with Glue or Adhesive:

If the new buttons don't stay securely in place, use a tube of instant glue or double-sided adhesive to secure them.

Functional Control:

Turn on the device and see if the new buttons are working properly. Make sure they have a clear answer and are properly recorded.

Reassembling the Device:

Reassemble the cover or case of the device by following the reverse steps of the disassembly kit.

Final Test:

Perform a full test of the device to ensure that all replaced buttons are working properly.

Important Notes:

Compatibility:

Be sure to purchase replacement buttons that are compatible with your device model.

Precision:

Work carefully to avoid damage to circuitry or other components during the replacement process.

Proper cleaning:

Clean the area thoroughly before installing the new buttons to ensure good contact.

Professional Replacement:

If you don't feel confident about dealing with replacing the buttons, consult a professional technician or service center.

Remember to also consult your device manufacturer's specific instructions, if available, to ensure accurate and safe replacement of physical buttons.

3.4.1 Power, volume, etc buttons

Replacing the power, volume, and other physical buttons on a device is an operation that may be necessary in the event of a failure or damage. Here's a general guide on how to deal with replacing these buttons:

Tools Needed:

Disassembly Kit:

Precision screwdrivers, opening spatulas and other necessary utensils.

New Replacement Buttons:

Make sure you have buttons that are compatible with your device model.

Antistatic tweezers:

Useful for handling components without damaging them.

Instant Glue Tube or Double-Sided Adhesive:

To attach the new buttons.

Button Replacement Procedure:

Turn off the Device:

Make sure the device is completely turned off before starting any replacement operations.

Removing the Cover or Shell:

Use the disassembly kit to remove the cover or case of the device. This may require the use of precision screwdrivers or opening spatulas.

Identifying and Removing Defective Buttons:

Identify faulty buttons (e.g., power, volume buttons) and remove them carefully. You may need to detach any connectors.

Cleanliness of the Zone:

Clean the area of debris from old buttons or any debris that may be interfering with the new buttons.

Installing the New Buttons:

Place the new buttons in their slots, making sure they are aligned correctly.

Fixing with Glue or Adhesive:

If the new buttons don't stay securely in place, use a tube of instant glue or double-sided adhesive to secure them.

Reconnecting Connectors (if necessary):

If you detached any connectors during removal, carefully reconnect them following the directions in the disassembly kit.

Functional Control:

Turn on the device and see if the new buttons are working properly. Make sure they have a clear answer and are properly recorded.

Reassembling the Device:

Reassemble the cover or case of the device by following the reverse steps of the disassembly kit.

Final Test:

Perform a full test of the device to ensure that all replaced buttons are working properly.

Important Notes:

Compatibility:

Be sure to purchase replacement buttons that are compatible with your device model.

Precision:

Work carefully to avoid damage to circuitry or other components during the replacement process.

Proper cleaning:

Clean the area thoroughly before installing the new buttons to ensure good contact.

Professional Replacement:

If you don't feel confident about dealing with replacing the buttons, consult a professional technician or service center.

Remember to also consult your device manufacturer's specific instructions, if available, to ensure accurate and safe replacement of physical buttons.

4   TROUBLESHOOT SOFTWARE

Troubleshooting software issues on devices such as Android phones and iPhones can involve several actions depending on the nature of the problem. Here's a general guide on how to deal with software issues:

1. Restarting Your Device:

A simple restart can fix many temporary issues. Turn your device off and on again.

2. Software Update:

Check to see if there are any operating system updates available. Install the latest versions to benefit from bug fixes and performance improvements.

3. Storage Control:

Make sure there is enough storage space on your device. Delete unnecessary apps or transfer files to an external storage device.

4. App Control:

Update apps to newer versions. If the problem persists, try uninstalling and reinstalling the affected app.

5. Clearing the Cache:

Clear the cache of your apps or operating system to delete temporary data that may be causing problems.

6. Check the Date & Time Settings:

Make sure your date and time settings are correct, especially if your device is connected to the internet.

7. Checking Network Connections:

Check your Wi-Fi or mobile data connection. If you're having trouble connecting, restart your router or data connection.

8. Battery Check:

If your device has performance issues when the battery is low, you may need to replace the battery or optimize the settings to save power.

9. Factory Reset:

This option should only be considered as a last resort. Factory reset deletes all data from the device. Be sure to make a backup before proceeding.

10. Check for Viruses and Malware:

- Use an antivirus app to run a full scan of your device and remove any threats.

11. Manufacturer's Support:

- If the problem persists, contact the manufacturer's support or visit an authorized service center.

12. Online Community:

- Search online forums or communities to see if other users have encountered similar issues and provided solutions.

13. Expert Consultation:

- If you can't solve the problem yourself, consult experts or specialized technicians.

Remember that the specific approach may vary depending on your device's operating system and the nature of the issue. Follow the guidelines provided by the manufacturer and be careful not to perform any actions that could further compromise the device.

4.1 Factory Reset

A factory reset is an operation that returns a device to its original condition when it was purchased by deleting all personal data, apps, and configurations made by the user. Here's how to perform factory reset on Android and iPhone devices:

Factory Reset on Android Devices:

From the Settings menu:

Access the "Settings Menu" on your Android device.

Scroll down and select "System" or "General" (this may vary depending on your Android version).

Tap "Reset" or "Backup & Restore."

Select "Factory Data Reset" or "Factory Reset".

You may be asked to confirm the process and enter your PIN or password.

Tap "Reset Phone" or "Reset Device."

Your device will restart and the reset process will begin. It will take some time.

Using the Physical Buttons (if the device does not boot normally):

Turn off your device.

Press and hold the power button and volume key at the same time.

Use the volume keys to navigate and the power button to confirm.

Select "Wipe data/factory reset" (or a similar item).

Confirm and start the recovery process.

Factory Reset on iPhone:

From the Settings menu:

Access the "Settings Menu" on your iPhone.

Tap "General."

Scroll down and select "Reset."

Tap "Erase All Content and Settings."

Enter your passcode if prompted.

Confirm the reset process.

Using iTunes (if your device doesn't boot normally):

Connect the iPhone to the computer and open iTunes.

Select your device in iTunes.

On the "Summary" tab, click "Restore iPhone."

Confirm the restore and wait for the process to complete.

Important Note:

Backup:

Before performing a factory reset, make sure to make a full backup of your data, as this will erase everything from your device.

Disabling Activation Lock (iPhone only):

If you have "Find My iPhone" turned on, you will need to turn it off before performing the factory reset.

Activating the Anti-Theft (Android only):

If you've turned on your alarm, you'll need to enter your Google Account credentials during the post-reset setup process.

Remember that factory reset is an irreversible procedure that erases all data from your device. Make sure you're sure you want to proceed before doing this.

4.2 Updating the operating system

Updating your operating system is an important step in ensuring that your device benefits from the latest features, bug fixes, and security improvements. Below, you'll find general instructions for updating the operating system on Android and iPhone devices:

Updating the Operating System on Android Devices:

Checking for Updates:

Access the "Settings Menu" on your Android device.

Scroll down and tap "System" or "About Phone."

Select "Software Updates" or a similar item.

Exhaust & Installation:

If an update is available, you'll follow the instructions to download and install the update.

Make sure you're connected to a Wi-Fi network, as updates can be large.

Rebooting Your Device:

After installation, your device may require a restart to complete the update process.

Updating the Operating System on iPhone:

Checking for Updates:

Access the "Settings Menu" on your iPhone.

Tap "General" and select "Software Update."

Exhaust & Installation:

If an update is available, tap "Download and Install."

You can choose to install the update now or later. If your device is connected to a Wi-Fi network, you can also set it to install automatically overnight.

Entering the Access Code:

During the installation process, you may be asked to enter your access code.

Acceptance of Terms:

Read and agree to the terms and conditions to proceed with the installation.

Rebooting Your Device:

Once the update is complete, your device will restart to apply the changes.

Important Notes:

Backup:

Before performing an OS update, it is always advisable to make a complete backup of your data to avoid the loss of important information.

Internet:

Make sure you are connected to a stable Wi-Fi network to avoid any interruptions while downloading the update.

Storage:

Check that there is enough storage space available on your device to download and install the update.

Duration of the Update:

Some updates may take some time. Make sure you have enough charge in the battery or connect your device to power during the update.

Carefully follow the instructions specific to your device and operating system during the update process.

4.2 Troubleshoot specific software issues (app crashes, system errors)

Troubleshooting specific software issues, such as app crashes or system errors, may require different approaches depending on the nature of the problem. Below, you'll find a general guide on how to deal with these situations:

1. App Crashes:

at. Force Close the App:

On Android: Go to "Settings" > "Apps" > [App Name] > "Force Close" or "Stop."

On iPhone: Double-click the Home button (or swipe up from the bottom on newer models) and swipe to the app you want to close.

b. Clear the App Cache:

On Android: Go to "Settings" > "Apps" > [App Name] > "Storage" > "Clear Cache."

On iPhone: Delete the app and reinstall it.

c. Update the App:

Check if there is an update available for the app and install it.

d. Restart Your Device:

A restart of your device can fix temporary issues that cause apps to crash.

2. System Errors:

at. Rebooting Your Device:

A restart can resolve many transient system errors.

b. Operating System Update:

Check to see if there is an OS update available and install it.

c. Clear System Cache:

On Android: Boot your device into recovery mode and select "Wipe cache partition."

On iPhone: You can't clear the system cache manually, but updating the operating system can improve performance.

d. Storage Control:

Make sure there is enough space on the device. Free up space by deleting unnecessary files.

and. Third-Party App Control:

Uninstall or update any third-party apps that may be causing conflicts or system errors.

f. Factory Reset:

This is an extreme option. Make a full backup of your data before proceeding.

3. Connection or Network Errors:

at. Internet Connection Control:

Make sure the device is connected to a stable Wi-Fi or mobile data network.

b. Rebooting the Router (if applicable):

If you're having trouble with your Wi-Fi connection, try restarting your router.

c. Configuring Network Settings:

On Android: Go to "Settings" > "Network & Internet" > "SIM Settings" > [Select SIM] > "Advanced" > "Cellular Network."

On iPhone: Go to "Settings" > "Cellular" > "Cellular Data Options" > "Reset Settings."

Important Notes:

Data Backup:

Before performing any actions that may cause data loss, make sure to make a complete backup of your device.

Device Specific Information:

Some devices may require specific procedures to resolve issues. Check the manufacturer's support or device documentation.

Support:

If you are unable to resolve the issue, contact the manufacturer's technical support or visit an authorized service center.

Online Community:

Look for device-specific online forums or communities to see if other users have encountered similar issues and provided solutions.

Follow the specific instructions for your device and operating system carefully during the troubleshooting process.

5   DATA RECOVERY

Data recovery depends on the nature of the problem and the type of data you want to recover. Here are some common options for data recovery:

1. Backup:

If you have a backup of the data, you can easily restore it to your device or a new device. Backups can be stored on cloud services such as Google Drive (for Android) or iCloud (for iPhone).

2. Data Recovery App:

There are data recovery apps available on Google Play Store for Android or App Store for iPhone. Some of these apps can help recover accidentally deleted photos, messages, and other data.

3. Data Recovery from Computer Backup:

You can use data recovery software on your computer to recover information from a backup previously created with iTunes (for iPhone) or with backup software on PC (for Android).

4. Professional Data Recovery Services:

If you have more complex issues, such as a damaged device or data lost due to a hardware malfunction, you may need to turn to professional data recovery services. There are specialized companies that offer this type of service.

5. Recovery from Cloud Services:

If your data was synced with a cloud service (e.g., Google Drive, Dropbox, iCloud), you can access those services from another device to retrieve the data.

6. Recover Deleted Photos and Videos:

Some apps or services offer the ability to recover deleted photos and videos, especially if they have been recently deleted. However, this may not work for all types of data.

Important Notes:

Add a Level of Protection:

After recovering data, consider implementing regular backup practices to avoid future loss of important information.

Avoid Overwriting Data:

Avoid saving new data to the affected device or storage before you have recovered the desired data. This reduces the risk of overwriting the data you intend to recover.

Remember that not all Data is Recoverable:

In some cases, especially if the data has been irreversibly overwritten or corrupted, it may not be possible to recover it.

Before Using a Professional Recovery Service:

Refer to the reviews and make sure you understand the fees and terms of service before committing to a professional data recovery service.

Consultation with Experts:

If you're not sure how to proceed, or if you're having complex issues, consult an expert or your device manufacturer's support.

Remember that the effectiveness of data recovery depends on many factors, so it's important to follow the specific instructions based on your situation and the type of data you want to recover.

5.1 Using Data Recovery Software

Using data recovery software can be an effective option for recovering files that have been accidentally deleted or lost due to software issues. Below, I give you a general guide on how to use data recovery software on a computer. Keep in mind that the steps may vary based on the specific software you're using.

General Guide:

1. Choose Data Recovery Software:

There are several options available, such as Recuva, EaseUS Data Recovery Wizard, Disk Drill, etc. Choose software that is reliable and suitable for your operating system (Windows, macOS, etc.).

2. Software Installation:

Download and install the data recovery software on your computer. Make sure to install the program on a different drive than the one you want to recover data from to avoid accidental overwrites.

3. Starting the Software:

Open the data recovery software. Some programs will have a wizard, while others may require you to manually select the options you want.

4. Location Selection:

Tell the software the location from where you want to recover data. It can be a hard drive, SD card, USB stick, etc.

5. Disk Scan:

Start scanning the disk. This process can take some time, depending on the size of your disk and the speed of your computer.

6. Examination of Results:

After scanning, the software will show the recoverable files. Carefully review the results and use the filter or search options to locate specific files.

7. Data Recovery:

Select the files you want to recover and indicate the location where you want to save them. Avoid saving the recovered files on the same location from where you are recovering them to avoid overwriting.

8. Complete the Process:

Wait for the software to complete the recovery process. Once done, verify the recovered files at the location you specified.

Important Notes:

Overwritten files:

If the files have been overwritten, it is possible that the recovery process will not return all the original data.

Storage of Recovered Files:

Save the recovered files on a different drive than the one from which you recovered them to avoid further data loss.

Backup:

Implement regular backup practices to avoid data loss in the future.

Read the Software Instructions:

Consult the documentation or instructions provided by the data recovery software for a complete understanding of its features and options.

Professional Recovery Services:

If the data recovery software fails to fix the problem, you may need to consult professional data recovery services.

Remember that successful recovery depends on the timeliness of the intervention and the nature of the data damage. If you have complex issues or concerns, it is advisable to seek assistance from professionals in the field.

5.2 Backup and Restore

Data backup and recovery are essential practices to ensure the safety of important information and to quickly restore a system in the event of data loss or device malfunction. Below, you will find a general guide on how to backup and restore on Android and iPhone devices.

Backup & Restore on Android Devices:

Data Backup:

Google Account:

Go to "Settings" on your Android device.

Select "Google" and then "Account."

Tap "Backup" and turn on the "Backup to Google Drive" option.

Manual Backup:

Some device manufacturers offer additional backup options. Go to the "Settings" > "System" > "Backup" and check the available options.

Data Recovery:

Google Account:

During device setup or after a factory reset, sign in with your Google account.

Choose "Restore from Backup" and select the desired backup.

Manual Backup:

If you've made manual backups, make sure you have access to the backup files and follow the manufacturer's instructions for recovery.

Backup & Restore on iPhone:

Data Backup:

iCloud:

Go to "Settings" on your iPhone.

Tap your name at the top and select "iCloud."

Tap on "iCloud Backup" and turn on the option. Tap "Back Up Now."

iTunes (on computer):

Connect the iPhone to the computer and open iTunes.

Select your device and go to the "Summary" tab.

In the "Backup" section, select "This Computer" and click "Back Up Now."

Data Recovery:

iCloud:

When setting up your device or after a factory reset, sign in with your Apple account.

Choose "Restore from iCloud Backup" and select the desired backup.

iTunes (on computer):

Connect the iPhone to the computer and open iTunes.

Select your device and go to the "Summary" tab.

In the "Backups" section, select "Restore Backup" and choose the backup you want to restore.

Important Notes:

Regular backups:

Make regular backups to ensure that you always have an up-to-date copy of your data.

Storage:

Make sure you have enough space on iCloud or your computer to make full backups.

App Sync:

Some apps may require a separate sync or may have built-in backup options. Check the settings of important apps.

Backup Photos & Videos:

For media files, consider using dedicated cloud services like Google Photos or iCloud Photos.

Selective Restore:

On both platforms, you can choose which data to restore during the device setup process.

Carefully follow the instructions specific to your device and operating system to ensure effective data backup and recovery.

6 PREVENTIVE MAINTENANCE

Preventive maintenance is a set of planned and proactive activities aimed at preserving functionality and extending the useful life of a device or system. Here's a general guide on preventative maintenance, with a focus on devices like smartphones and computers:

Preventive Maintenance for Smartphones:

1. Software Updates:

Keep your operating system and apps up-to-date to benefit from security fixes, new features, and optimal performance.

2. Physical Cleanliness:

Use a soft cloth to clean the screen and body of the device. Make sure the ports and connectors are free of dust and debris.

3. Storage Management:

Delete useless files, uninstall unnecessary apps, and transfer photos and videos to an external storage device or cloud services.

4. Regular Backups:

Make regular backups of important data to avoid loss of information in the event of a device failure or loss.

5. Battery Check:

Monitor the status of the battery and replace it if necessary. Avoid completely discharging the battery regularly.

6. Protection from External Elements:

Use protective covers and screen films to protect your device from bumps, scratches, and dust.

Computer Preventive Maintenance:

1. Software Updates:

Keep your operating system, drivers, and antivirus software up-to-date to ensure optimal security and performance.

2. Interior and Exterior Cleaning:

Clean your computer of dust using compressed air. Make sure the cooling fans are clear of obstructions.

3. Storage Management:

Delete unnecessary files, defragment your hard drive (if necessary), and consider using an SSD to improve performance.

4. Regular Backups:

Make regular backups of important data to external devices or cloud services.

5. Asset Tracking:

Use resource monitoring tools to identify and resolve any performance issues.

6. Temperature Control:

Monitor your computer's temperature to prevent overheating. Make sure the fans are working properly.

7. Hardware Upgrade:

Upgrade hardware components such as RAM or hard drives if necessary to improve performance.

Important Notes:

Planning:

Perform preventative maintenance on a regular basis, following a set schedule.

Proper Storage:

Store devices in an environment with controlled temperature and humidity.

Electrical Overload Protection:

Use electrical overload protections to prevent damage due to power surges.

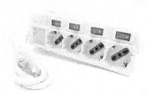

Manufacturer's Advice:

Follow the guidelines provided by the manufacturer for maintaining your device.

Preventive maintenance helps prevent problems and extends the useful life of your devices while reducing the risk of data loss or sudden malfunctions.

6.1 Cleaning Computer Components

Cleaning components is an essential part of preventative maintenance to ensure the proper functioning and longevity of devices. Below, I provide guidance on cleaning components for computers and smartphones:

Cleaning the Components

1. Screen:

Use a soft cloth to clean the monitor screen. Moisten it lightly with water if necessary, avoiding too aggressive solutions.

2. Keyboard:

It uses compressed air to remove dust and debris between the keys. You can also use a soft-bristled toothbrush or a low-powered vacuum cleaner.

3. Central Unit (CPU):

Turn off your computer and turn off the power.

Use compressed air to remove dust from the heat sink and fans. Make sure the airflow is not obstructed.

4. Ports and Connectors:

Clean the USB, HDMI, and other connectors with compressed air or cotton swabs soaked in isopropyl alcohol.

5. Heat Sinks:

Make sure the heatsinks on your video cards and other components are dust-free to ensure optimal cooling.

6. Power Cord:

Inspect the power cord for any damage and clean it carefully.

7. Computer Case:

Wipe the outside of the case with a dry cloth. If necessary, you can use a damp cloth, but avoid getting water inside.

Cleaning Smartphone Components:

1. Screen:

Wipe the screen with a microfiber cloth. To remove stubborn stains, you can use a small amount of water or a 50% isopropyl alcohol solution.

2. Protective Cover:

Remove the protective cover and wipe it with a cloth. Clean the back of your phone as well.

3. Connectors:

It uses compressed air to remove dust and debris from connectors such as the charging port and audio jack.

4. Earphone and Microphone Jack:

Check and clean the earphone jack and microphone with a slightly damp cotton swab.

5. Speakers:

Use compressed air gently to remove dust from the speakers.

6. Cleaning the Case:

Wipe the phone case with a damp cloth. Avoid the use of harsh solvents.

Important Notes:

Turn off devices:

Before you start cleaning, turn off your computer and smartphone and turn off the power.

Compressed air:

Use compressed air with caution and keeping a safe distance to avoid damage to components.

Avoid excess fluids:

Avoid using excess liquids when cleaning. If necessary, lightly dampen the cloth.

Cleaning Materials Control:

Make sure that the cleaning materials are not harsh and do not damage the device.

Regular cleaning of components helps maintain a safe working environment and prevent devices from overheating. However, be careful not to damage the components during the cleaning process.

6.2 Regular Software Update

Regularly updating your software is a crucial aspect of ensuring the optimal performance, security, and reliability of your device. This practice is applicable to computers as well as smartphones and other electronic devices. Here are some general guidelines for updating your software regularly:

Updating the Software on Computer:

1. Operating System:

Make sure to install OS updates regularly. Both Windows and macOS provide security updates and performance improvements on a regular basis.

2. Device Drivers:

Update your device drivers, especially those related to graphics cards, sound cards, and input/output devices. You can do this manually or use auto-update tools.

3. Security Software:

Keep your anti-virus and anti-spyware software up to date. Virus definitions should be updated regularly to ensure effective protection.

4. Installed Programs:

Regularly check to see if there are any updates available for programs installed on your computer, including browsers, productivity suites, and other third-party software.

5. Device Firmware:

If you're using devices with upgradable firmware (such as routers, printers, or webcams), check the manufacturers' websites for firmware updates.

Software Update on Smartphone:

1. Operating System:

Be sure to install operating system updates provided by Google for Android or Apple for iOS. These updates include security improvements, bug fixes, and new features.

2. Applications:

Enable automatic app updates or manually check the App Store (for iOS) or Google Play Store (for Android) to install individual app updates.

3. Device Firmware:

Some Android devices may require the manufacturer's firmware update. Check the manufacturer's official website for updates.

4. Security:

Use antivirus software (especially on Android devices) and keep it up-to-date with the latest virus definitions.

5. Backup & Restore:

Before making any major updates, make a full backup of your data to avoid the loss of important information.

Important Notes:

Internet:

Make sure you are connected to a stable network during upgrades to ensure their success.

Proper nutrition:

During updates, make sure your device is sufficiently charged or connected to power.

Periodic Inspection:

Manually check for updates every once in a while, especially if you've disabled automatic updates.

Reboot after upgrade:

After installing important updates, restart your device to ensure that the changes are fully applied.

Regularly updating your software is crucial to ensure the optimal security and performance of your device. Keeping your operating system and applications up-to-date will help you benefit from the latest features and protect yourself from potential security vulnerabilities.

6.3 Using Protective Cases and Films

Using protective cases and films is an effective way to preserve the physical integrity and smooth functioning of devices such as smartphones, tablets, and other electronic devices. Here's how you can get the most out of protective cases and films:

Protective Cases:

Shock & Fall Protection:

Protective cases, especially reinforced ones, offer a barrier against bumps and drops. Choose a case that covers the corners and sides of the device.

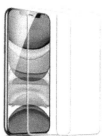

Resistant Materials:

Opt for cases made of impact-resistant materials such as polycarbonate, TPU (thermoplastic polyurethane), or silicone.

Display Protection:

Some cases are designed with raised edges to protect the screen when the device is placed face down.

Slim or Robust Design:

Choose a case according to your aesthetic preferences. Some are slim and unobtrusive, while others offer more robust protection.

Easy Access to Ports:

Make sure the case allows easy access to the charging ports, audio jacks, and other connectors.

Film Compatibility:

Make sure your case is compatible with the use of protective films on the screen and back of your device.

Protective Films:

Screen Protector:

Screen protectors offer a barrier against scratches, fingerprints, and dust.

Transparent Materials:

Opt for films made of high-quality transparent materials so as not to compromise the clarity of the screen.

Anti-glare or Anti-Blue Light:

Some films offer anti-glare or anti-blue light capabilities to reduce eye strain.

Precise Application:

Be sure to apply the film without air bubbles and precisely so as not to compromise the quality of the screen.

Front and Back Films:

If you want complete protection, consider using films for both the screen and the back of the device.

Easy to Clean:

Choose a film that is easy to clean and repels fingerprints to maintain a cleaner screen.

Important Notes:

Regular Maintenance:

Regularly check the condition of your cases and films. Replace any that are damaged or worn.

Compatibility:

Make sure the cases and films are compatible with the specific model of your device.

Accurate Installation:

Follow the film installation instructions carefully to avoid air bubbles or trapped dust.

Periodic cleaning:

Clean the cases and films periodically to remove dirt, dust, and residue.

Using protective cases and films is a worthwhile investment in keeping your device in optimal condition over time, reducing the risk of damage and preserving its value.

7 ADDITIONAL RESOURCES

7.1 Useful Links

Here are some additional resources that may be helpful for more information about servicing, repairing, and using electronic devices:

Maintenance and Repair of Electronic Devices:

iFixit:

iFixit provides step-by-step repair guides for a wide range of devices, including smartphones, computers, tablets, and more.

YouTube:

Look for video tutorials on YouTube for your device's specific maintenance and repair. Many people share their experiences and helpful tips.

Technical Support Forums:

Join technical support forums such as Stack Exchange, Tom's Hardware, or XDA Developers to get advice from experts and enthusiasts.

Learning Resources:

Khan Academy:

Khan Academy offers free online courses on a variety of topics, including those related to technology and computer science.

Coursera:

Coursera provides high-quality online courses on a wide range of topics, including those related to computer science and electronics.

Software Troubleshooting Resources:

TechSpot:

TechSpot provides news, reviews, and guides on hardware, software, and electronic devices.

Microsoft Support:

Microsoft Support provides resources and guides for troubleshooting issues related to the Windows operating system.

Apple Support:

Apple Support is the official technical support resource for Apple devices, providing guides and solutions to common issues.

Online Community:

Reddit:

There are several communities on Reddit dedicated to technology, electronics, and problem-solving. For example, r/techsupport and r/electronics.

GitHub:

GitHub is a collaborative development platform that hosts many open-source projects. You can find resources and solutions to common problems.

Stack Overflow:

Stack Overflow is a developer community where you can ask questions and get answers to programming and software development problems.

Always remember to check the validity and reliability of sources and follow safety practices when performing maintenance or repairs on your devices.

7.2 Recommended Video Tutorials

Here are some recommended YouTube channels and video tutorials that might be helpful in learning further about maintaining, repairing, and using electronic devices:

YouTube Channels:

iFixit:

iFixit is known for its detailed repair guides. The YouTube channel offers video tutorials on various repairs and hardware upgrades.

JerryRigEverything:

This channel is managed by Zack Nelson and focuses on endurance testing, repairs, and teardowns of various devices.

Linus Tech Tips:

Linus Sebastian offers reviews, PC build guides, and content related to hardware and technology.

Dave Lee:

Dave Lee provides in-depth reviews on laptops, smartphones, and other electronic devices.

TheUnlockr:

The TheUnlockr channel provides tutorials on modding, unlocking, and customizing smartphones and other devices.

Specific video tutorials:

How to Fix a Water Damaged Phone:

Tutorials on how to deal with water damage on electronic devices.

How to Replace a Laptop Screen:

Guide on how to replace a damaged laptop screen.

iPhone Battery Replacement Guide:

Tutorial on how to replace an iPhone battery.

How to Upgrade Your RAM:

Guide on how to upgrade RAM on a computer.

How to Build a Gaming PC:

Tutorial on how to build a gaming PC.

Remember to check the release date of these videos, as technologies and procedures can evolve over time. Additionally, be sure to follow the manufacturer's instructions and take appropriate safety measures during any maintenance or repair activities.

7.3 Online Technical Support Communities

If you're looking for online tech support communities, there are several platforms where you can get help from tech experts and enthusiasts. Here are some popular online communities:

Stack Overflow:

Stack Overflow is a developer community where you can ask questions and get answers on a wide range of topics related to software development and programming.

Super User:

Super User is a section of Stack Exchange dedicated to computer and technology enthusiasts. You can ask questions about software, hardware, and more issues.

Tom's Hardware:

Tom's Hardware is a forum that covers a wide range of topics, including hardware, software, gaming, and more. It's a good place to get advice on technical issues.

XDA Developers:

XDA Developers is a community dedicated to developers and advanced users of Android devices. You'll find discussions about modding, unlocking, and custom software development.

TechSpot:

TechSpot is a community of tech enthusiasts that discusses hardware, software, gaming, and more. The forum offers technical support and discussions on a wide range of topics.

Reddit - TechSupport:

Reddit's TechSupport subreddit is a place where users can ask questions about technical issues and get advice from other members of the community.

Reddit - Electronics:

Reddit's Electronics subreddit is dedicated to discussing electronics topics, including DIY projects and technical questions.

BleepingComputer:

BleepingComputer is a forum that offers malware removal support, as well as discussions about cybersecurity, hardware, and software.

Microsoft Community:

The Microsoft Community is a place where you can get official support for Microsoft products, including Windows and Office.

Apple Support Communities:

Apple Support Communities are dedicated to Apple device users and provide a place where you can get help and exchange information.

Remember to respect the individual communities' guidelines and rules, and provide all necessary information when asking for help to maximize your chances of getting helpful answers.

8 CONCLUSIONS

8.1 Summary

In summary, if you are looking for technical support online, you can turn to several specialized communities. Some of the major platforms include:

Stack Overflow: Developer community for questions and answers about programming and software development.

Super User: A section of the Stack Exchange dedicated to questions about technology, hardware, and software.

Tom's Hardware: A forum that covers topics such as hardware, software, and games.

XDA Developers: A community dedicated to developers and advanced users of Android devices, with a focus on modding and unlocking.

TechSpot: A community of tech enthusiasts discussing hardware, software, and games.

Reddit - TechSupport: Reddit subreddit dedicated to questions about technical issues.

Reddit - Electronics: Reddit subreddit dedicated to electronics discussions, DIY projects, and technical questions.

BleepingComputer: A forum that offers malware removal support and discussions about cybersecurity, hardware, and software.

Microsoft Community: Official support for Microsoft products, including Windows and Office.

Apple Support Communities: A community for Apple device users to get help and share information.

Remember to follow the rules and guidelines of each community, and provide clear details when asking for help to get helpful answers.

8.2 Encouragement for DIY

Absolutely! DIY is a fulfilling activity full of opportunities to express creativity and gain new skills. Here are some words of encouragement for your DIY journey:

Be curious:

"Every project starts with a question. Be curious, explore, and learn new things. DIY is your playground to satisfy your curiosity."

Experience without fear:

"Don't be afraid to experiment! Some of the best results come from experiments and trials. Every 'mistake' is a learning opportunity."

Persist in challenging moments:

"Remember that every challenge is just one more step towards success. Perseverance is the key to DIY. Don't give up when things get tough."

Creativity is Personal:

"Your creativity is unique and personal. There is no single right answer in DIY. Do what you're passionate about and you'll always find satisfaction."

Celebrate Small Successes:

"Every step forward is a success. Celebrate small progresses and don't underestimate the satisfaction of seeing the fruits of your labor."

Share with the community:

"The DIY community is an incredible place to learn, share ideas, and get support. Don't hesitate to share your projects and ask for advice."

Learn continuously:

"Do-it-yourself is a continuous learning journey. Every project is an opportunity to acquire new skills and improve."

Be Proud of Your Work:

"No matter the size of the project, take pride in your work. Everything you create is a unique piece that brings your own personal touch."

Embrace Imperfection:

"Imperfection is an integral part of DIY. Don't strive for absolute perfection, but enjoy the process and the unique character that each project brings."

Enjoy:

"DIY should be fun and rewarding. Don't forget to have fun along the way. The joy you feel in creating is one of its most precious aspects."

Whether you're working on small projects or big DIY adventures, remember that every step counts and that your commitment is an inspiration to others and to yourself. Happy DIY!

Start of Module